Design ALL AROUND US

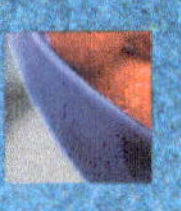

By Jan Anderson

Design All Around Us

Text: Jan Anderson
Design: Karen Mayo
Illustrations: Karen Mayo
Editor: Sally Green
Photographs: Lindsay Edwards
Typeset in: Stone Serif
Reprint: Siew Han Ong

Acknowledgements
Photgraphs by Alessi, p. 10 right, cover; Australian Picture Library, p. 22 bottom/ Corbis/ Bettmann, pp. 18 top, 18 bottom, 19 top right/ Bob Krist, p. 6 bottom/ Lee Snider, p. 12 top/ Peter Harholdt, p. 20 bottom; City-Link, p. 15 bottom; Coo-ee Picture Library, pp. 19 bottom right, 21 right; CopperLeife, p. 14 top; Danish Design Centre, pp. 9 bottom left, bottom right cover; Getty Images, p. 7 top right/ Hulton Archive, pp. 13 top left, 19 top left/ Image Bank, pp. 7 top left, 8 bottom/ Photdisc, pp. 6 top, 20 top/ Rob Melnychuk, p. 7 bottom/ Stone, p. 20 centre; Kosta Boda Bildbank, p. 17 bottom; Masterfile/ Lloyd Sutton, p. 14 bottom; Newspix, p. 19 bottom left; Photo Edit/ Garry Connor, p. 9 top; Photolibrary.com/ Digital Stock Imagery, p. 15 top; Picture Source/ Terry Oakley, pp. 5 bottom, 19 bottom right, cover; Select Kitchens, p. 13 top right.

PM Plus Non Fiction
Emerald
Looking at Art
Get the Picture?
Getting the Message
Design All Around Us
Dancing to the Beat
Music Technology

ISBN 978 0 17 009913 4
ISBN 978 0 17 009911 0 (set)

Cengage Learning Australia
Level 7, 80 Dorcas Street
South Melbourne, Victoria Australia 3205
Phone: 1300 790 853

Cengage Learning New Zealand
Unit 4B Rosedale Office Park
331 Rosedale Road, Albany, North Shore NZ 0632
Phone: 0800 449 725

For learning solutions, visit **cengage.com.au**

Printed in Australia by Ligare Pty Ltd
19 20 21 22 23 24 25 25 24 23 22 21

Contents   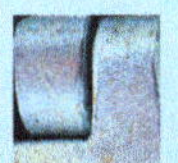

CHAPTER 1

What Is Design?

Although you might not stop to think about it, design affects you almost every minute of the day.

Design is how things are made or put together, how they look, how they work and what they do. Almost everything you use has been designed before it was made — from the lids on bottles to the chairs we sit on.

If something is badly designed, it does not work well or may not last for a long time.

This jug keeps liquids hot or cold. It is attractive to look at, strong, and works well, too, because it is designed not to drip.

Technology plays a big part in design. Computers are used to help design new products.

Technology can also help us make new materials that are friendly to the environment; for example, special **plastics** that can be recycled. Designers can create many new things with these materials.

A well-designed object can be very beautiful. It will also be safe and easy to use. Good design makes our everyday lives easier and more enjoyable.

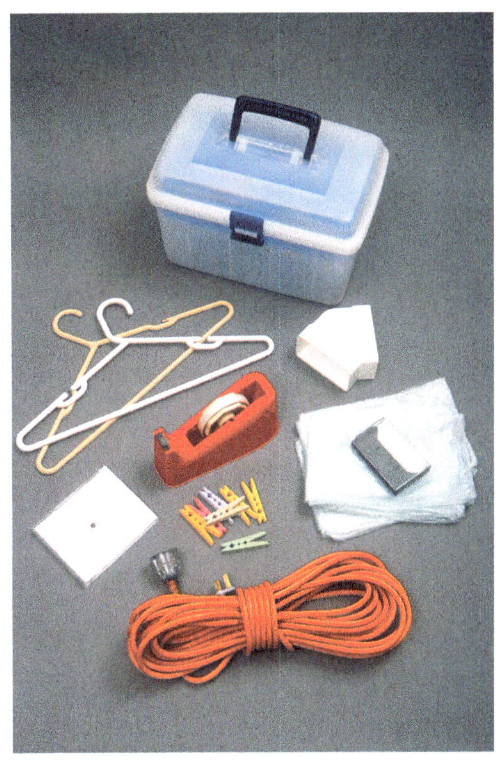

Recycled plastic products

DID YOU KNOW?

In many countries, awards are given each year for well-designed products.

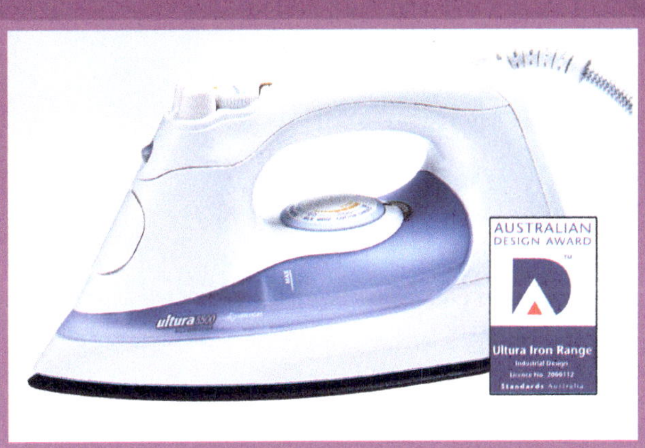

CHAPTER 2

Technology and Design

During the last century, designers have been able to create many new products. Often this has been because of new technology.

New materials

Plastic is a material made possible by technology.

Designers like using plastics because they are strong and can be made in bright colours.

Plastics can also be **moulded** into many shapes. We can make spoons, chairs, or just about anything from plastics.

Granules of plastic are poured into moulds and melted to make a range of objects. The melted plastic becomes a solid shape when it cools.

Silicon is an important new material. It is used to make **silicon chips**. Before the silicon chip was invented, small radios and computers could not have been designed. The parts were too big!

New processes

Technology has produced many new **processes**, like chrome-plating. Chrome-plating is a process in which a coating of chrome (a kind of metal) is put on another metal — usually steel. The chrome protects the steel from rusting. Chrome is also very shiny, which makes it a beautiful material to use.

This kitchen tap has been chrome-plated.

CHAPTER 3

Design in the Home

Look around your home: a lot of thought has gone into designing things to make them look good and work well.

The food processors, computers, tables and chairs that your family uses were probably all made in a factory. But they all had to be designed first.

'Classic' designs, such as this alarm clock, are always popular because they look good and work well.

Chairs

Chairs are designed for people to be comfortable when they are seated. Probably more people have tried to design a chair than any other piece of furniture!

Some chairs are for relaxing in.

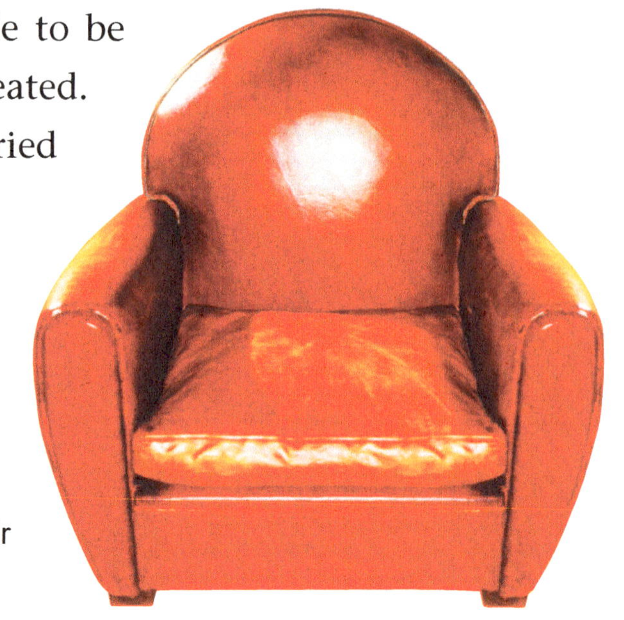

A comfortable chair

Other chairs are designed for people to sit on while they are working at their desks. These chairs need to be upright and must allow people to sit with a good **posture**.

This chair has been designed to support your back when you sit at a desk.

DID YOU KNOW?

There have been many famous chair designs. Some are named because of their shapes, such as the Swan and the Egg chairs.

The Egg chair

The Swan chair

In the kitchen

Everyone likes a kitchen with an oven that is easy and safe to use, or a spoon that stirs well. It makes cooking easier, faster and more enjoyable.

Over the years, new technology has changed the kitchen a lot.

Alessi is a company which makes many beautiful and practical kitchen goods. At first sight, you might not know that this kitchen tool is made for squeezing lemons and oranges.

The first toasters were designed with an open heating element. Later, doors were added on the sides to protect your hands from the element. You opened the doors to put the bread inside. From time to time, you had to check to see that the bread was not burning, and turn the bread over to cook the other side.

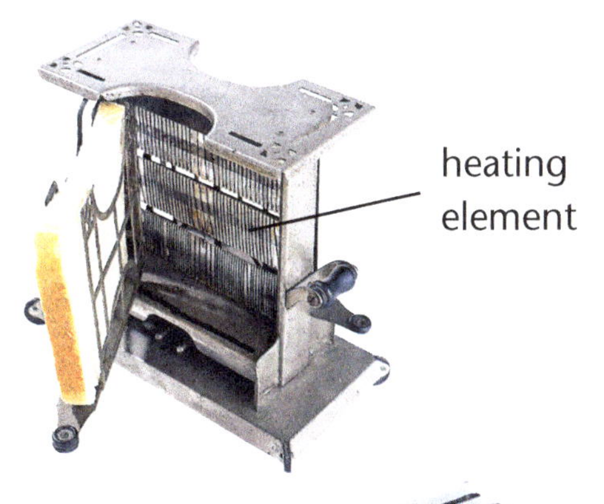

Today's toasters are **automatic**. You drop the bread in the top, and when it is cooked, it pops up.

DID YOU KNOW?

In the 1950s, the control panels on some stoves were made to look like those in cars. Designers did this because they thought that the cars' control panels were very stylish.

CHAPTER 4

Design Outside

Homes

Hundreds of years ago, houses had very simple designs. They were often made of stone and had small windows, because glass and curtains were expensive. They were dark, and cold in winter. The only heating was from wood fires. These houses were not designed for comfort because people had so few materials to build with.

An old house

Modern houses are designed so that we have a good quality of life. Many houses today have **open-plan** living, which provides more living space. Some houses have windows that open onto a garden.

A modern house design

Today's houses are built of materials such as brick, steel and concrete. They are designed for comfort. They have stoves that heat up as soon as they are turned on, and hot water available from a tap.

An old kitchen

A modern kitchen

DID YOU KNOW?

You can buy automatic outdoor blinds that are designed to sense when the wind is strong. When it is very windy, the blinds roll up so they are not damaged.

Designs that are friendly to the environment

Today, **architects** design homes that use less electricity and are kinder to the environment. These houses are more **energy-efficient**.

This **solar** water heater is a good way of using nature's energy to heat water in the home, instead of using electricity.

New houses also have **insulation** in the roof and walls. This helps keep houses warm in winter, and cool in summer, so air conditioners and heaters aren't needed as much. This means that less electricity or gas is used.

DID YOU KNOW?

Architects use computers to help them design a house. Computers can draw **three-dimensional** pictures of the inside.

Design in public places

Design is also very important in public places. In some cities there are **malls**. These are streets that are designed to be free of traffic — people can walk safely, without having to think about cars.

Today's **urban planners** know that safety is important when designing, or changing, cities.

Many freeways now have barriers designed to protect nearby homes from the noise of cars. These barriers are designed to look nice, too.

This modern sound barrier helps protect apartment blocks from traffic noise.

CHAPTER 5

Scandinavian Design

Scandinavia is a group of countries in Europe that is famous for its designers, and for producing excellent design.

IKEA® is a furniture shop that began in Sweden.

IKEA® uses world-famous designers to design its products, and make good design available to the general public.

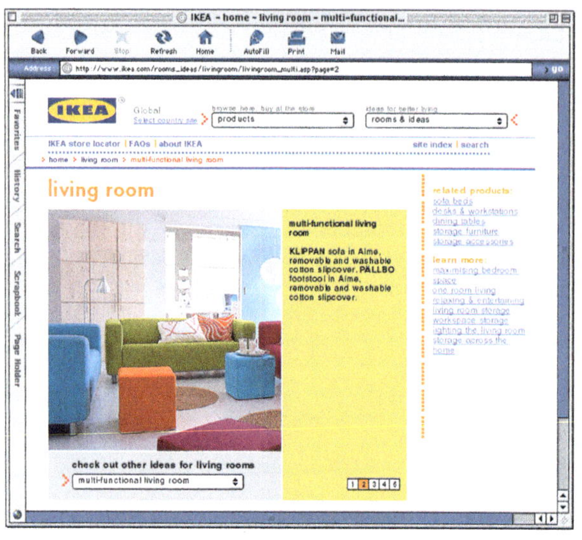

Many IKEA® products come in separate pieces. Customers follow instructions to put them together at home.

IKEA® furniture is displayed in a catalogue and on the Internet.

Lego™ was invented in Denmark. The man who invented it was a **carpenter**. The first toys he made were formed out of wood. But, he wanted to make a toy that could be used again and again, so that children could keep playing with it in many different ways.

Later, he designed Lego™ bricks that were made of plastic. Plastic was a good material for making bricks that would snap together easily, and not fall apart.

DID YOU KNOW?

In Sweden, people have been designing and making glass objects for nearly 300 years. These objects are both beautiful and useful.

 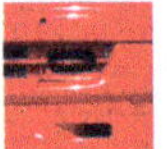 

CHAPTER 6

Car Design

The design of cars has changed a lot over the years. This timeline shows some important dates in car design, from the first car until today.

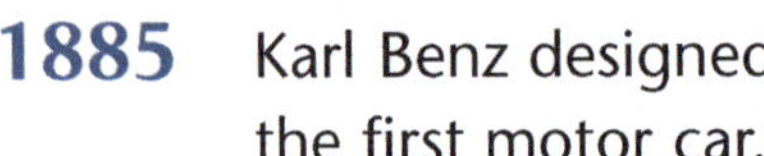

1885 Karl Benz designed the first motor car.

1913 Model T Fords were **mass-produced**. This cut down the time it took to make cars, which meant they cost less.

Henry Ford said: "You can have any colour you like, as long as it's black!" This also helped to keep the price low.

1920s General Motors began to make new styles of car every year. They also made cars in many colours. Both these things encouraged people to buy new cars.

1934 Chrysler designed a car that was very **streamlined**. It copied the shape of the planes and trains of the time.

1940 General Motors made the first fully automatic cars. People no longer had to change gears themselves.

1959

Everyone loved the Mini because it was a small family car that was cheap to buy and did not use a lot of petrol.

1998 Volkswagon's 'new beetle' is a copy of an old design that was very popular.

There is a vase for flowers inside.

2000

This 'green car' was designed in Australia. It is friendly to the environment because it does not need much fuel.

Bumper bars

The design of bumper bars has changed many times since the first car was invented. This is because car designers are always finding new and better materials to use in their designs.

The first bumper bars were made of steel that was painted to stop it from rusting.

Later, steel bumper bars were covered in chrome to stop rust forming. Because chrome is shiny, designers also loved the look of it.

Today, most bumper bars are made of a type of plastic that crumples when a car is hit. This protects the rest of the car better than older kinds of bumper bars.

DID YOU KNOW?

The first cars had no plastic in them, but we couldn't imagine a modern car without lots of plastic.

CHAPTER 7

Packaging Design

There are many people who work in **packaging** design. Supermarkets are full of packages. These packages help to sell the product. They also protect what's inside.

Packaging is often brightly coloured, or has an unusual shape.

Most bottles are made of green, brown or clear glass. This drink bottle is made of blue glass so that we notice it. This helps sell the brand of drink.

However, most packaging is designed in the shape of a box. Boxes are easy to pack and carry. They can be easily stacked on the shelves of a shop, or in our cupboards at home.

The cardboard carton may not be as beautiful as some containers, but it will not break if you drop it. What's more, the whole package can be used as a label, to tell us what's inside.

DID YOU KNOW?

The Body Shop uses bottles that are designed to be refilled, instead of thrown out. The company knows that '**green design**' looks after the environment.

Lids for drink containers

There are many designs for the lids of drink containers. Here are some of them.

A simple cork is an easy way to seal a bottle. It is designed to go inside the bottle.

The screw-top was developed in Britain about 150 years ago. It is designed to go over the neck of the bottle.

The crown top, or crown **seal**, was first designed and made about 100 years ago, in America.

Drink cans have a metal ring. When the ring is pulled, it folds back into the can so it cannot be swallowed or dropped.

This cardboard cask has its own tap through which the drink flows. You can open and close the tap as many times as you like.

Drink containers can also have holes for straws, or even spouts to pour from.

Glossary

architect	a person who designs buildings
automatic	when something works by itself
carpenter	a person who makes things from wood
energy-efficient	uses the smallest amount of energy possible
granules	small, hard pieces
green design	design that is friendly to the environment
insulation	material that protects against heat and cold
mall	a street for people, but not traffic
mass-produced	made at factories in large amounts
moulded	made in a particular shape
open-plan	a style of building with very few walls inside
packaging	protective covering like cardboard or gloss
plastics	a kind of material that comes from oil
posture	how we sit, stand or walk
processes	ways of making things
seal	a kind of lid
silicon	an element found in rocks, and used to make **silicon chips**
silicon chips	tiny electronic parts made of silicon, and used in computers
solar	power from the sun
streamlined	designed to move easily through air or water
three-dimensional	when something has depth, width and height
urban planner	a person who designs cities and towns

Websites

To view famous designs in furniture, vases, clothes, dishes and many other things, go to these websites:

Chicago Athenaeum, Museum of Architecture and Design.
http://www.chi-athenaeum.org/gdesign/gdesign0.htm

Cooper-Hewitt National Design Museum at the Smithsonian Institution NYC.
http://ndm.si.edu/COLLECTIONS/index.html

Australian Design Awards. **www.designawards.com.au**

www.design-council.org.uk

Index